DAVE'S BAD JOKES

Dave Moore is a radio presenter, podcast host and music producer. His Today FM morning show is the biggest commercial music radio show in Ireland. He is also passionate about sneakers, languages, guitars and DIY. Dave lives in Portmarnock with his wife, the artist and illustrator Tracy Sheridan, and their four children.

DAVE'S BAD JOKES

DAVE MOORE

GILL BOOKS

Gill Books
Hume Avenue
Park West
Dublin 12
www.gillbooks.ie

Gill Books is an imprint of M.H. Gill and Co.

© Dave Moore 2024

978 1 80458 206 0
Design and layout by Liz White Designs
Edited by Jane Rogers
Proofread by Paula Elmore
Printed and bound in the UK using 100% Renewable Electricity at CPI Group (UK) Ltd
This book is typeset in League Gothic.

The paper used in this book comes from the wood pulp of sustainably managed forests.
All rights reserved.
No part of this publication may be copied, reproduced or transmitted in any form or by any means, without written permission of the publishers.
A CIP catalogue record for this book is available from the British Library.

5 4 3 2

INTRODUCTION

I'm Dave. And I love bad jokes! And good jokes! And great jokes! I love all jokes!

About 15 years ago, I thought it would be funny to read out some pretty bad jokes on my radio show to my co-host, Dermot. He laughed at some, groaned at most and then we played a song. During that song, our text machine exploded with messages from people who loved the jokes and wanted to tell me their jokes. And so Dave's Bad Jokes was born.

It's been on my radio show every week since then, and when I got my very own show, *Dave Moore* on Today FM, it grew to not one but two slots per week.

I must thank my amazing listeners. They send me hundreds of jokes every week and I keep them all in a HUGE joke book, each one painstakingly hand-drawn like the Book of Kells. Nah. They're on my computer. That was just a joke. The jokes in the book are better. Well, some of them are.

I scoured my hard drive full of jokes and chose the best ones to include in this book. There are some about animals, space and food but I took out the one about the pancake. To be honest, I told it at the book launch, and it fell a bit flat. Come on!

If you've made it this far into the introduction, you've probably read all the jokes and come back to this bit to see were there any jokes in here. One more so: did you hear about the radio DJ who released a joke book? He ... Oh, sorry. I can't finish it. I've hit the maximum word count. If I didn't write that, I probably could have typed the punchline. Ah well.

Love,

Dave

I once dated an archaeologist, but
I had to break up with him.
He just kept digging up the past.

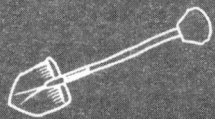

My sister applied for a new job recently. In her interview the employer asked, 'How flexible are you?' She replied, 'Well, I used to do gymnastics!'

I told my therapist that I'm scared of the 15th, 9th and 3rd letters of the alphabet. He replied, 'Oh, I see,' which didn't help.

My mate was fighting in the Bricklayers'
White Collar Boxing event last night.
He won! The other corner threw in the trowel.

> I just opened my new fridge, and it stinks of basil. I think it's faulty!

I just asked my wife, 'If you won the lottery, would you still love me?' She said, 'Of course I would. I'd miss you, but I'd still love you.'

I just got a bar installed into my roof so that when people come over, I can say 'drinks are on the house!'

What do you call a group of Scottish goats?

A billy colony!

> My wife thinks I overanalyse our marriage, which, to be frank, completely contradicts the findings of my report.

A lad I met in the bookies today told me to put all my money on a horse named Landfill. Turns out it was a rubbish tip.

My friend rushed into the bar and shouted, 'Mate! I just saw your car getting stolen, but don't worry, I got the reg!'

My wife is blaming me for ruining her birthday. That's ridiculous, I didn't even know it was her birthday!

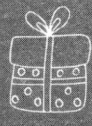

How can you tell how heavy a red-hot chilli pepper is?

Give it a weigh, give it a weigh, give it a weigh now!

A coach full of old jazz musicians has broken down on the M50, blocking two lanes. Gardaí say to expect lengthy jams.

I get paid weekly ... very weakly!

I'm really bad at delegating. I usually just get someone else to do it for me.

I make apocalypse jokes
like there's no tomorrow!

People who say 'Go big or go home!' are seriously underestimating my willingness to go home. It's literally all I want to do.

Did you know that King Kong's full name is Kingsley Konglington?

I bought some chicken drumsticks earlier today. Now I just need a chicken that plays the drums.

— ∙∙∙ —

A man has been arrested after falling into farm machinery while trying to steal it. He is due to be bailed next Friday.

— ∙∙∙ —

> Don't bother phoning the tinnitus helpline. It just keeps ringing.

**Have you ever tried blindfolded archery?
You don't know what you're missing.**

I once bought a wooden car. Wooden engine, wooden doors, wooden wheels, wooden seats. I put the wooden key in the wooden ignition. Only problem? Wooden start.

I went to the tanning Olympics. I got bronze.

I'm giving up drinking for a month.
Sorry, bad punctuation.
I'm giving up. Drinking for a month.

I was in the reptile enclosure in Dublin Zoo the other day and there was a lizard standing on its hind legs and it was telling jokes! I asked the keeper what kind of lizard it was. He said, 'It's not a lizard, it's a stand-up chameleon.'

I hate it when people act all intellectual and go on about loving Mozart when they haven't even seen one of his paintings.

> During my interview today, I poured out a glass of water and it overflowed a bit onto the table. 'Nervous?' asked the interviewer. I simply replied, 'No. I just always give 110 per cent.'

I grilled a chicken for an hour last night.
He still wouldn't tell me why he crossed the road.

I went to the supermarket with my wife, and she had the cheek to call me lazy. I was so shocked I nearly fell out of the trolley!

After I gave my dad his fiftieth birthday
card, he said to me, 'You know, son,
one would have been enough!'

We bought some glow-in-the-dark dog treats for our two Jack Russells.
You should see their little faeces light up!

I stormed in and shouted at my wife, 'Hey! Did you eat my chocolate eclair in the fridge?' She just looked at me and said, 'Nah, I ate it in the living room.'

I bought a greyhound today.
My wife said, 'Are you going to
race him?' I said, 'God, no way,
Sheila. He's much faster than me.'

Did you hear what happened
to my uncle Tommy?
He evaporated!
Ah, he'll be mist.

We were waiting for our luggage at the airport, but someone stole my bag – all that came round on the carousel were the wheels and the handle. I told my wife, 'I'm going to report it to the police.' She said, 'I don't think you've got much of a case.'

My daughter's hamster escaped from his cage last night. I spent four hours looking for him. He definitely wasn't in the pub!

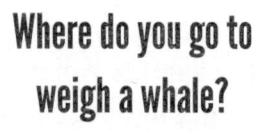

Dogs can't operate MRI machines.
But CAT scan.

**How did the chicken cross the road so quickly?
She was wearing Reebok-bok-boks!**

Which animal has the most memory?

The RAM.

What do alpacas worry about?
Llamageddon!

What do llamas worry about?

The Alpacalypse!

My uncle called his Dobermanns Timex and Rolex. They're watch dogs.

Fitness instructor: Have you ever done a marathon?
Me: On Netflix?

My wife said she's leaving me, due to my obsession with The Monkees. I thought she was joking. But then I saw her face ...

I answered the door this morning and a six-foot-tall beetle punched me in the face and called me an idiot. Apparently, there's a nasty bug going round!

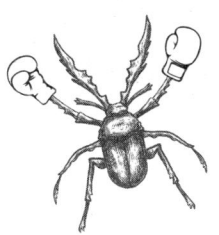

Scientists have found that cows produce more milk when the farmer talks to them. It's a case of in one ear and out the udder!

My grandfather used to say, 'Back in my day, I could go into a shop with two pounds, and I'd come out with a loaf of bread, a dozen eggs, butter and still have some coins in my pocket. But these days, they have bloody cameras everywhere!'

My wife said she's leaving me because of my huge ego. I said, 'Yeah, right, love. Close the door on the way back in.'

My husband went into the attic and found a photo of himself back in his boxing days. If you turn it sideways it looks like he's standing up.

My wife thinks she's better than me at bird-related puns. Well, toucan play that game.

My horse will only come out of her stable when it gets dark. She's becoming a bit of a night mare.

My wife asked me if I could clear the kitchen table. I had to get a running start, but I made it.

Just read a few interesting facts about frogs. They were ribbiting!

— ... —

I went onstage with my band and said,
'Hi folks, we're called The Subtractions!
Take it away, boys!'

— ... —

What do you call an underwater dog?

A subwoofer!

I've been using my U2 sat nav for weeks and it's bloody useless. The streets have no name, and I still haven't found what I'm looking for!

My racing snail kept losing so I took
off his shell to speed him up.
If anything, it's made him more sluggish.

Is anyone else having problems with nuisance phone calls? My most common one seems to be, 'You said you'd be home from the pub three hours ago!'

What did Beyoncé say to the girl who lost her balloon?

'If you liked it then you should have put a string on it!'

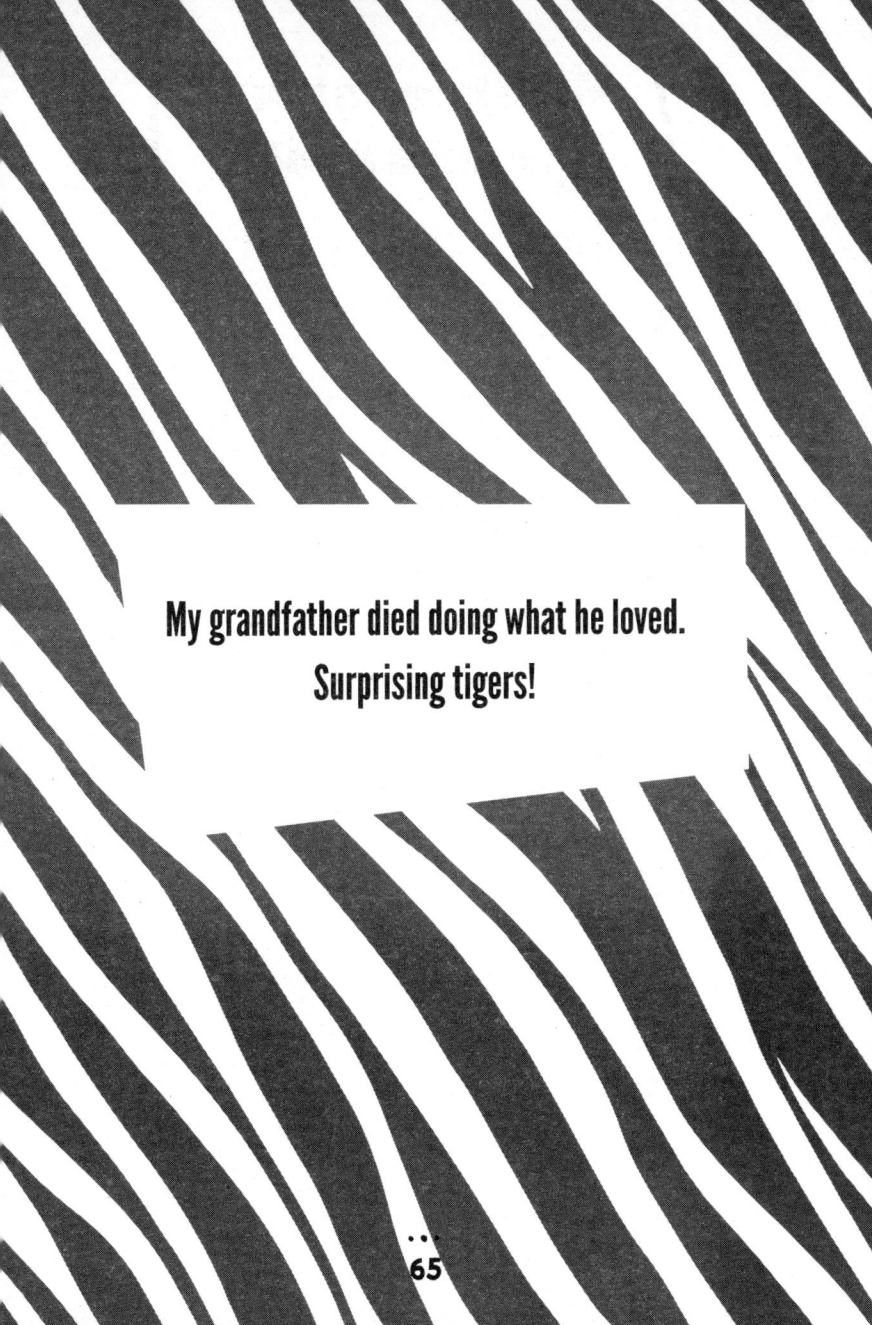

Where's the best place in America
to shop for a football kit?
New Jersey.

Did you know that Johnny Cash used to work in Dublin Zoo? It's true! He used to walk the lion.

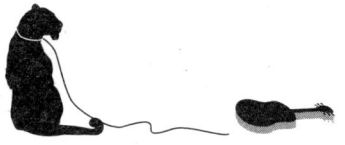

> Nobody believed me when I told them that I'm a singer in a Black-Eyed Peas tribute band. Well I am!

It's sad, but a butterfly that gets addicted to drugs becomes a crystal moth.

Did you hear there's a virus going around that's making people forget bands that started in the '80s? Nobody knows The Cure!

Did you hear the fire alarm
went off in IKEA this morning?
We all had to self-assemble in
the car park.

I always carry a picture of my wife and kids in my wallet. I do it to remind myself why there is no money in there.

Billy Joel was sacked from his local chipper because he didn't start the fryer.

I'm not saying my wife orders a lot from Amazon but if I got a job as a delivery driver, they'd probably let me work from home.

My wife videoed herself during the entire process of having her hair done. Apparently, she wants to watch the highlights later!

My new bed plays Metallica
to help soothe me to sleep.
Nothing else mattress.

My girlfriend just couldn't accept my obsession with horoscopes. In the end, it Taurus apart.

Couldn't work out why Genesis and The Beatles never got together to form a supergroup and then I realised what they would be called ...

I wondered why the tennis ball was getting bigger.
Then it hit me.

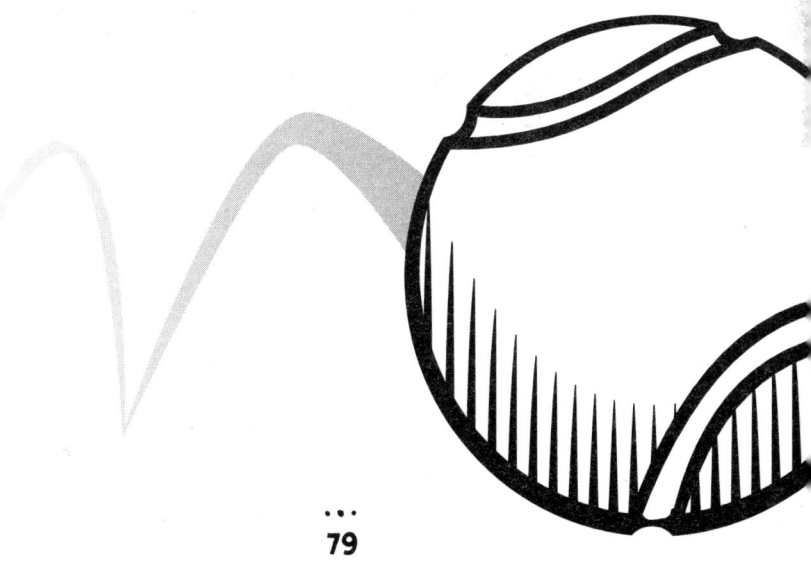

What do you get when you mix a flower shop and a football club?

Nottingham Florist.

Husband: How many degrees should I set the washing machine at?

Wife: What does it say on the T-shirt?

Husband: Er ... Pink Floyd.

I'm not saying I'm bad at betting, but I backed a horse last week at ten to one. It came in at a quarter past four.

My boss yelled at me this morning, 'Hey! This is the fourth time you've been late to work this week! Do you know what that means?' I said, 'Yep. It's Thursday.'

Little Johnny gets called up by the teacher, who says, 'Now, the essay you wrote about your dog is the same, word for word, as the essay your brother in sixth class wrote.'

'Of course it is, miss, it's the same bleedin' dog!'

I once entered the kleptomaniac championships.
I took gold, silver and bronze.

I'm actually making use of my gym membership this New Year. I spent 45 minutes on one machine this morning, until it finally ran out of KitKats.

I just quit my job at the Halls Soothers factory. So long, suckers!

Paddy was devastated when his dog went missing. His wife suggested he put an ad in the paper. A week later, Paddy's still upset because there hasn't been a single answer. His wife asks him, 'What did you put in the ad, Paddy?'
'HERE, BOY! CLICK CLICK! HERE, BOY!'

{ I have a question.
If I eat cake fast enough,
will my Fitbit think I'm walking? }

If laziness was an Olympic sport, I'd come in fourth so I wouldn't have to walk up to the podium.

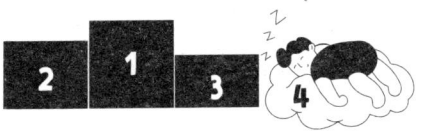

My dad was bragging about his new
state-of-the-art hearing aid.
'Cool,' I said. 'What type is it?'
'Five past six,' he replied.

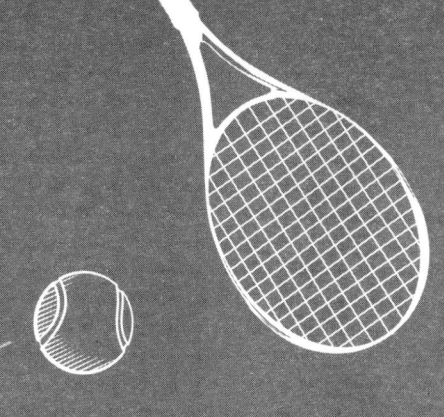

The man who invented the automatic tennis serving machine is celebrating his birthday today. Many happy returns!

I've been dropped from my limbo dancing team.
I'm so annoyed. I bent over backwards for them.

My grandad warned people the *Titanic* would sink. No one listened, but he kept warning them until they got sick of him and kicked him out of the cinema.

People started calling me a cheat after I won yesterday's charity fun run. Me? I was so shocked I nearly fell off my bike!

What do you call a gangster Llama?

Al Pacacino.

I can't seem to find my *Gone in 60 Seconds* DVD. I really don't know why as I only put it down a minute ago.

Have you heard of the new Netflix show where a guy breaks into homes and heats up food in the microwave? It's called *Stranger Pings*.

I was in the pub with five of my mates. Six of us sitting around chatting and they told me they thought I was tight with money. Me? I was shocked!
To prove them wrong I bought them a pint. Turns out they wanted one each.

I dunno about you, but I reckon the maddest thing about the Last Supper is the fact that 13 lads in their 30s were all free for dinner on the same night.

Yesterday one of my good friends told me
I often make people uncomfortable by violating
their personal space. It was a really hurtful
thing to say and completely ruined our bath.

 They say music can take you places. Today, for example, they put country music on and I  went to the next bar.

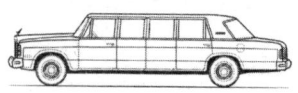

I've been a limo driver for 25 years and
I've never had a single customer.
All that time and nothing to chauffeur it.

What's the most groundbreaking invention ever?

The shovel!

I started a new job today. The first thing my boss did was give me five euro to go down to the hardware store and buy, wait for it, a glass hammer, a bubble for a spirit level and a tin of tartan paint. I said, 'Do you really think I'm that stupid? All that is going to cost way more than a fiver!'

I've opened a shop selling uncaged birds.
They are flying off the shelves!

— ... —

Guy walks into a bar with a set of jump leads around his neck. Barman looks at him and says, 'You can come in, but you'd better not start anything.'

— ... —

A woman walks into a library and asks if they have any books about paranoia. The librarian leans forward and whispers, 'They're right behind you!'

I have a Polish friend who's a roadie for a band.
I have a Czech one too. Czech one too.

Did you hear what they started calling Pat the Baker after he retired? Pat.

Just graduated after three years at clown college. No small feet!

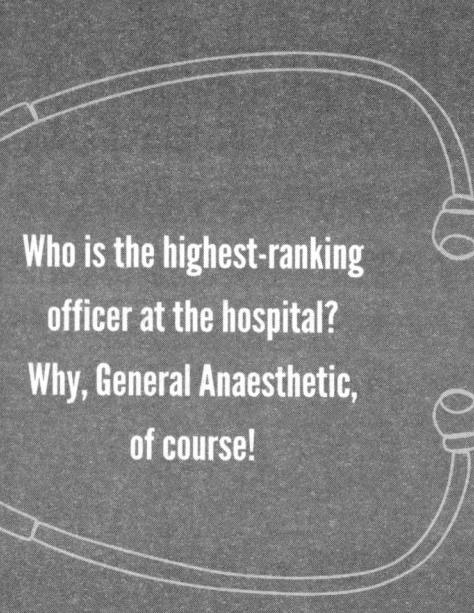

Who is the highest-ranking officer at the hospital? Why, General Anaesthetic, of course!

Pat was going for his first-ever job on a building site, so he went into the prefab to talk to the foreman. The foreman asked, 'Well, Pat. Can you make tea?'

'Oh, I can, yeah,' says Pat.

Then the foreman asks, 'Can you drive a forklift?'

'Well, hang on a minute,' says Pat. 'How big is the fecking teapot?'

Is it okay that I start drinking as
soon as the kids get to school?
Or does that make me a 'bad teacher'?

I'm a dancer and people forget that during the pandemic I had to twerk from home.

I was getting on a packed bus earlier and the driver said, 'Sorry, mate, I'm full. You're gonna have to wait for the next one.' I asked, 'Any idea how long it'll be?' and he replied, 'Same length as this one!'

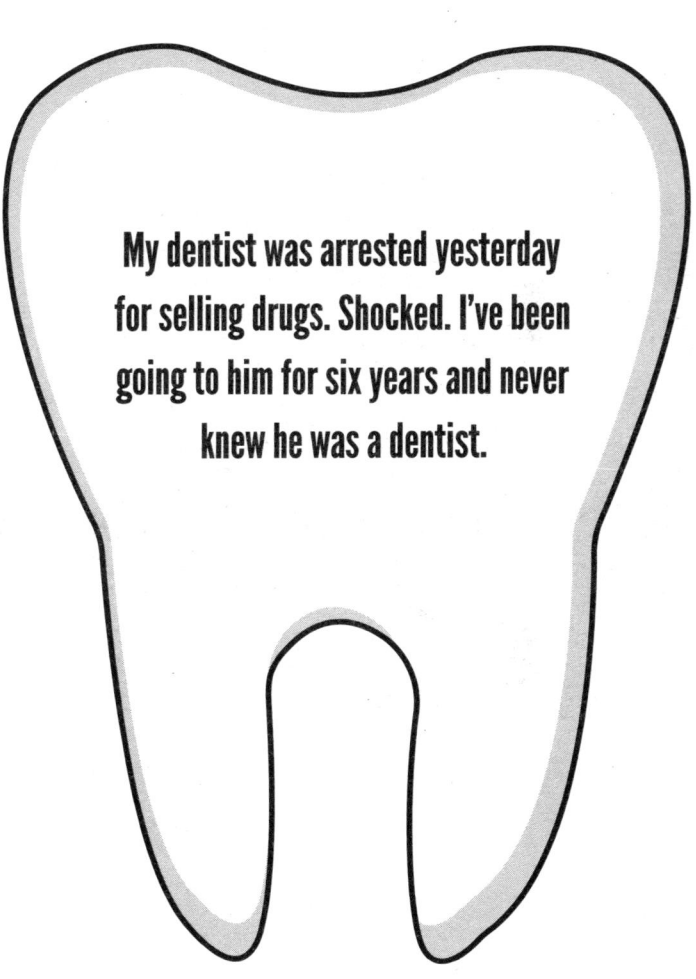

— ... —

My wife claimed she was late coming home tonight because she was ambushed by a group of elderly men who pinned her down and repaired her shoes. Sounds like a load of old cobblers to me.

— ... —

I used to work as a programmer for autocorrect.
Then they fried me for no raisin.

A Dutchman has invented shoes that record how many miles you've walked. Clever clogs!

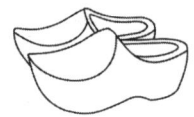

Did you hear about the
restaurant on the moon?
Great food, no atmosphere.

I went into the library and asked,
'Do you have a book called *Pantomime Jokes*?'
She whispered, 'Yep. It's behind you!'

I'm no conspiracy theorist,
but you can't deny it,
every eclipse is just a big cover-up!

I have perfected my recipe for a soup made entirely from ingredients extracted from the atmosphere. It's a broth of fresh air!

I had to quit my job at the watch factory.
The man sitting opposite me kept making faces.

I'm working on overcoming my addiction
to marshmallows, chocolate and nuts.
I'll be honest, it's a rocky road.

You know when you buy a bag of salad leaves, and it goes brown and soggy? You know what never does that? Doughnuts. Just sayin'!

Did you hear about the person who had his fruit basket stolen? He was left peachless.

My girlfriend left me because I'm too insecure.
No, wait she's back!
She was just making a cup of tea.

I baked a giant chocolate eclair yesterday, but I couldn't finish it. I'd bitten off more than I could choux.

Why does Mr Tayto have a phone?

In case Johnny Onion rings.

What do you call an Irish lad who breaks up fights?

Liam Malone!

What do you call an alligator wearing a vest?

An investigator!

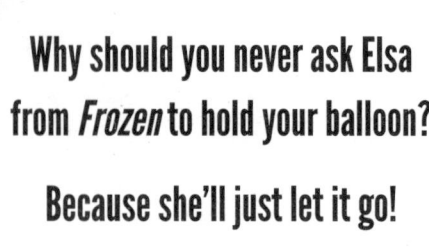

Why should you never ask Elsa from *Frozen* to hold your balloon?

Because she'll just let it go!

A lorryload of tortoises crashed into a trainload of terrapins. What a turtle disaster!

What did the bee say when she returned from a long trip?

Ah, hive, sweet hive!

What do you call an old snowman?

A puddle.

Why was the broom late for the meeting?

It overswept!

I think I'll sleep on my husband's side of the bed tonight. Apparently from that side you don't hear the kids wake during the night.

'I need a new bum.'
'Eh, really? Why?'
"Cos my old one has a crack in it!'

After spending an hour unclogging the bathtub and sink, I'll be honest, I'm feeling pretty drained.

When it comes to messing up simple sayings, I've been there, done that, bought the teabag ...

Isn't it true that Vikings believed in reincarnation? Does that mean they were all Bjorn again?

I just found out that 'Bottomless Brunch' referred to the unlimited food and drink and not the dress code.

What's the opposite of irony?

Wrinkly!

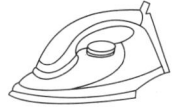

Ninety per cent of people are bad at maths.
I'm glad I'm in the other 20 per cent.

In the tooth-brushing competition, there was a gold medal for first place but everyone else got plaque!

I've deleted all the Germans I know from my phone contacts. Now it's Hans-free!

Would you believe it? After three years of therapy, they cancelled my final anger management session without telling me! I've never been so mildly irritated in my life!

I'm writing a book about all the things I should be doing in my life. It's called *My Oughttobiography*.

People say the grass is always greener on the other side. But I turned mine over and it was just brown with worms in it.

I had eczema, diarrhoea and haemorrhoids last weekend. It was my best game of Scrabble ever!

I'm very upset. Someone broke into our house and stole my favourite coffee cup last night. Now I have to go to the Garda station and look at mugshots!

A little bit of friendly advice. No matter how good the soap smells in public toilets, never walk back out of there sniffing your fingers!

**My calculator is missing the minus button.
On the plus side it still works.**

Before I begin, I'd just like to test this microphone.
Can anyone named Michael please stand up?
One, two, three of you.
Okay, this concludes the Mike check!

{ I've recently started to leave the door open when I go to the toilet. I'll be honest, I'm getting some weird looks at traffic lights. }

I'm all for colouring books.
But dot-to-dot books?
That's where I draw the line.

I put my motorbike for sale in Autotrader. Someone asked, 'What's the lowest you could go on it?' I said, 'About five km/h. Any slower and you'll fall over.'

I shall fight for the right to identify as a Smurf until I'm blue in the face!

I went to a guy who said he'd cure my sore back by pouring 7Up and Fanta on it. It sounds a bit mad, but I think this fizzy-otherapy is actually working.

I've got no problem with genetically modified food.
Just had a lovely leg of salmon.

Some fella just offered me a free gate. I said: 'What's the catch?' He said: 'It's the bit that allows it to open and close ...'

Apparently, Madeira is one of the most difficult airports in which to land, but my friend is a pilot, and he reckons it's a piece of cake.

Last night someone broke into our house and took a dozen eggs. They also left a saucepan filled with warm water. Gardaí believe it was poachers.

My Eiffel Tower knowledge is very limited. I know it's 330 metres tall and that's about the height of it.

I had surgery on my funny bone yesterday. The surgeon said I'd be in stitches for three weeks!

A vegan said to me that people who sell meat are disgusting. I said, 'Yeah, well, people who sell fruit and vegetables are grocer!'

Do you ever wake up, kiss the person sleeping beside you and just feel glad that you are alive? Well, I just did and apparently I'm not allowed on this train any more.

Where do sharks go on holiday?

Finland.

**Where do vegetarians go on holiday?
Quornwall.**

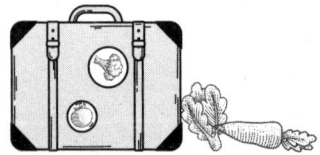

www.conjunctivitis.com.
Now that's a site for sore eyes.

I ordered a chicken and an egg off Amazon.
I'll let you know.

> Cosmetic surgery used to be such a taboo subject. Nowadays, you can talk about Botox and nobody raises an eyebrow.

I was going to make myself a belt made out of watches, but then I realised it would be a waist of time.

I just started reading a horror novel in Braille.
Something really bad is about to happen,
I can just feel it.

I was visiting Argentina, but I was shocked at how cold it was. In fact, it was bordering on Chile.

I've just been to my allotment, and someone has added more soil to it again. The plot thickens.

My car failed its emissions test today ... fuming.

How do you get
Pikachu on the bus?
Pokémon.

A Vicks VapoRub truck overturned on the M50 this morning. Amazingly, there was no congestion for eight hours.

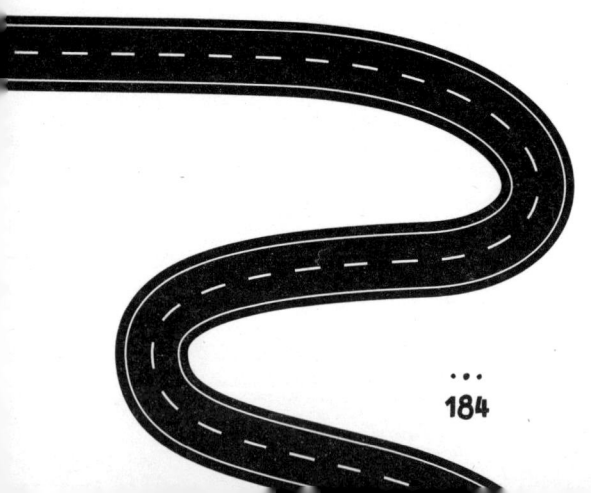

Lance is an uncommon name nowadays. But in medieval times people were called Lance a lot.

Some breaking traffic news ...
The M7 is blocked after a lorry shed its load of brightly coloured writing paper, butterfly stickers and *My Little Pony* envelopes.
Gardaí say the traffic is pretty stationery.

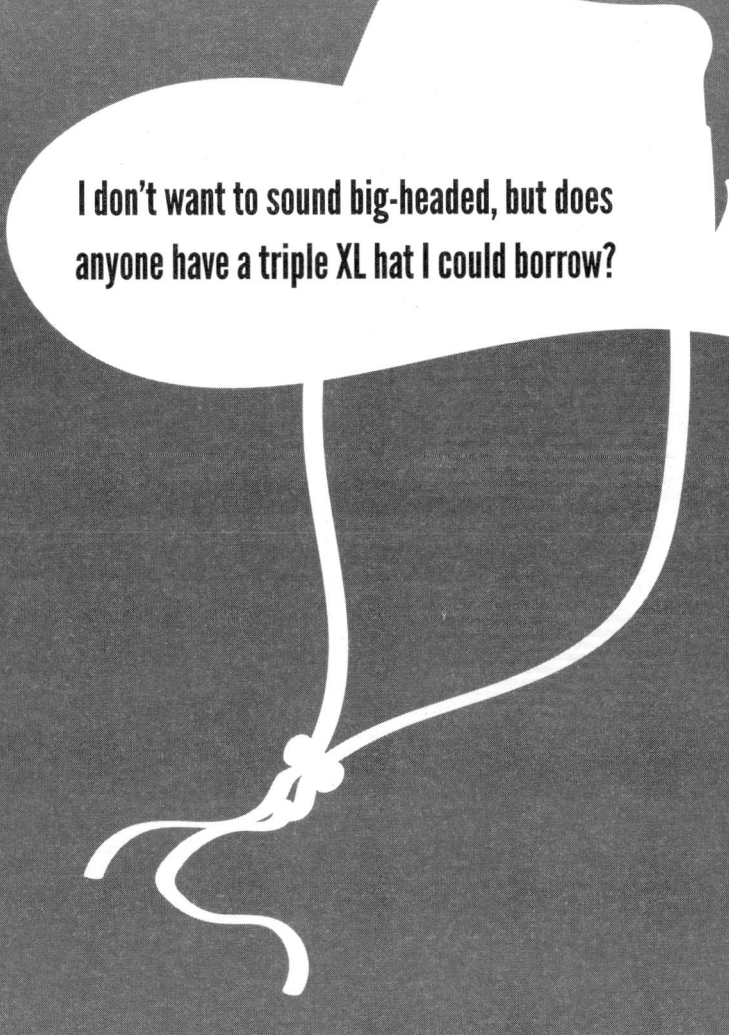

I don't understand why some people lie about their age. I love being 37 and I've loved it for ten years now.

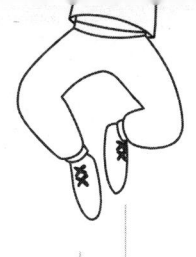

To save electricity I've wired
my electric toaster to my
electric blanket.
Now I just pop out of the bed!

I wish people would stop using the same word twice in a sentence. It really annoys me. Enough is enough.

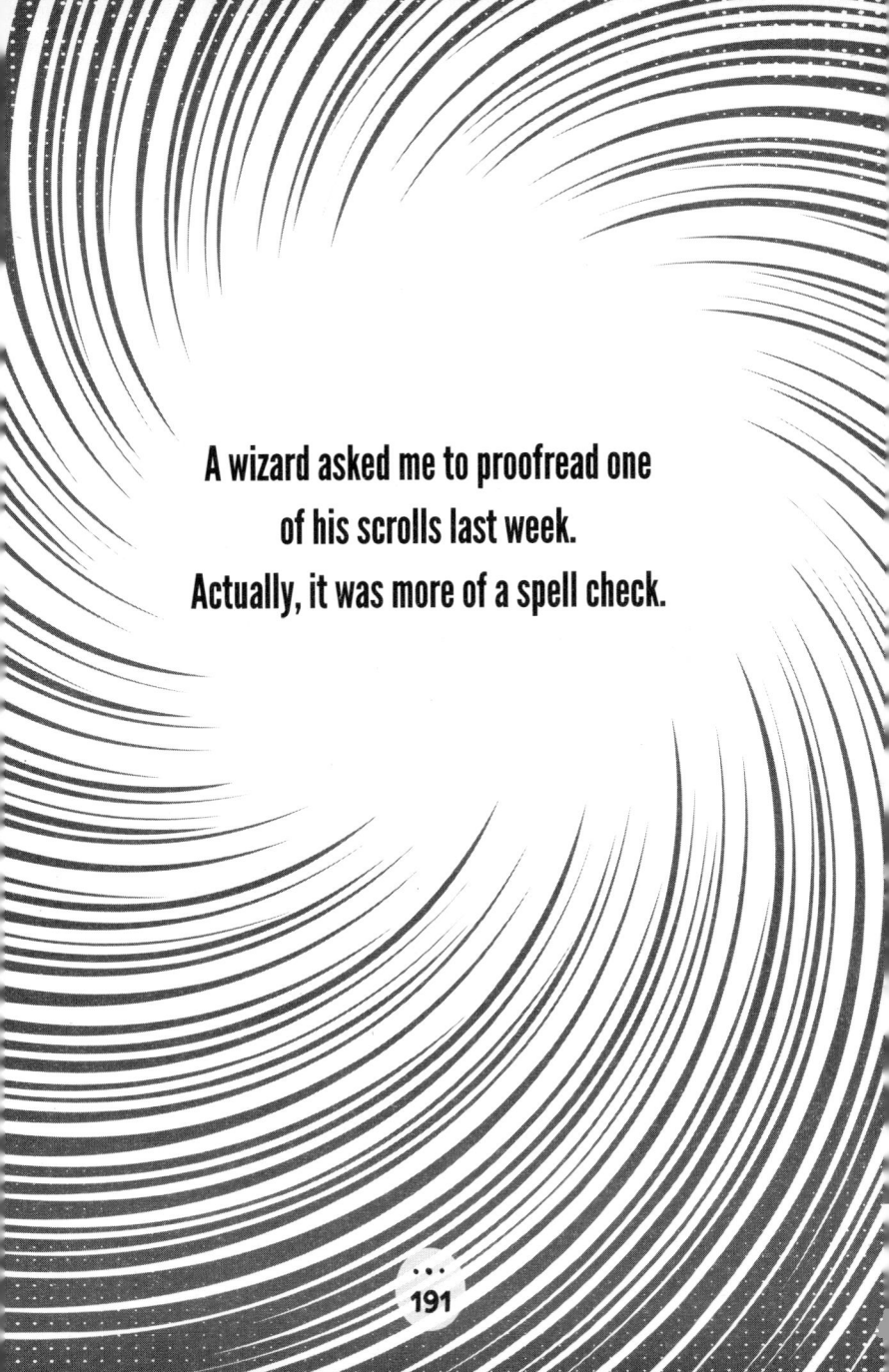

I've been reading a book about the history of paper towels. It's very absorbing.

— ∙∙∙ —

**Have you been sold badly made, substandard double glazing?
If so, you could be entitled to condensation.**

— ∙∙∙ —

 The mythological half-man half-horse was a total show-off. I think he just wanted to be the centaur of attention.

I'm getting worried about my addiction to batteries. I might start attending AAA meetings.

I went to the doctor yesterday and told him that every time I cough, I hear words like knight, queen, bishop and pawn. He said I had a chess infection.

If you're being chased by a pack of taxidermists, don't ever play dead.

Bought myself some animal biscuits today but I couldn't eat them. The seal was broken.

How does a French
skeleton say hello?
Bone-jour!

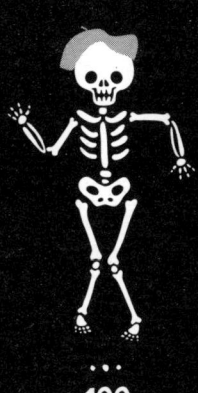

I asked seven billionaires, 'What's the secret to your success?' and they all said the same thing: 'How did you get into my mansion?'

Just paid twenty euro for a two-mile taxi drive to the launderette. Not happy. Really feel like I've been taken to the cleaners.

I accidentally drank a bottle of invisible ink last night. I'm now in hospital, waiting to be seen.

I didn't realise I was such a bad driver until my sat nav said, 'In 400 metres stop and let me out.'

I asked my friend when their birthday was. He said March 1st. So I got up, stomped around the room and asked again!

I'm not saying I'm attractive, but when I take my clothes off in the bathroom, I turn the shower on.

For my next trick I intend to eat a percussion instrument sandwich. Drum roll, please!

Just got called pretty today! Well, the full statement was, 'Hey! You're pretty annoying,' but I like to focus on the positive.

People said I'd never get over
my obsession with Phil Collins.
But take a look at me now!

To the person who stole my barbecue rotisserie last night ... what goes around comes around!

**Apparently, my snoring is so loud
I scare everyone in the car I'm driving.**

I've just spent my entire life savings on pasta.
It was worth every penne.

I just found out after twenty years that my father was a mime. He never said a word about it.

I'm looking to hire a chef who is very frugal with herbs. No thyme wasters please.

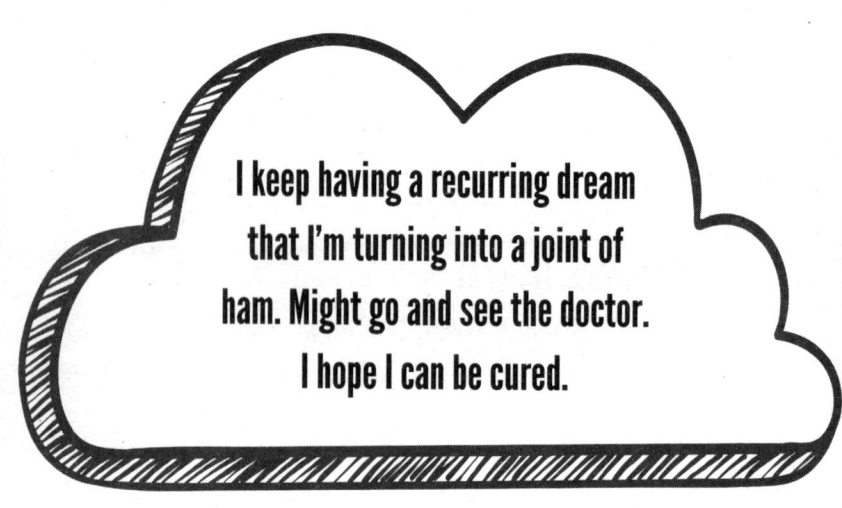

I keep having a recurring dream that I'm turning into a joint of ham. Might go and see the doctor. I hope I can be cured.

I once went out for a meal with a bunch of electricians. None of them wanted starters; they just went straight for the mains.

I've been up at 6 a.m. with my trainer every day this week. If I find the other one, I might go for a jog!

— ∙∙∙ —
My memory has got so bad now I reckon I could organise a surprise party for myself.
— ∙∙∙ —

My wife and I are having a boy.
We're thinking of naming him Saturn.

It has a nice ring to it.

Yesterday I went to the world's tiniest wind turbine exhibition. Honestly, not a big fan.

Just bought a bargepole.
Thought I'd push the boat out.

Engineers have just made a car that runs on parsley. Next, they're working on a bus that runs on thyme.

What do you call a teacher who's always late?
Mister Bus!

What do you call a woman with the *Titanic* on her head?
Mandy Lifeboats!

I bought some robotic garden shears today.
They are cutting-hedge technology!

Why did the man get fired from the orange juice factory?

He couldn't concentrate.

Why did the same fella get fired from the pasta factory?

Fusilli mistakes.

My buddies and I are opening a chiropractor business. We're calling it the Back Straight Boys.

Just found out I've failed
my German exam.
Sacré bleu!

Would I be worried if someone fired questions at me all about Stallone movies? Not in the Sly test!

My wife says I have a habit of always making things up. I mean, in fairness, I don't even have a wife.

I came first in a dungaree-wearing competition.
You could say I was the overall winner.

Deaf sheepdogs. They're hard to come by.

I was kidnapped by a mad scientist who experimented on me, replacing my limbs with animal ones. If I ever see him again, I'll tear him apart with my bear hands.

What's small, red and whispers?

A hoarse radish.

On the subject of podiums,
where does everyone stand?

...
236

Whenever I think of the '80s, I think of a boom box.
But I suppose that's just a stereo type.

Where do you go for help
with your nut allergy?

Cashewlty!

My wife is threatening to leave me
because of my constant puns about Africa.
Kenya believe that?
Really Ghana miss her if she goes.

I accidentally spilled some household cleaner on sensitive work documents. I'm now being sued for bleach of contract.

At a young age I was adopted by a man called Daz or, as I used to call him, my non-biological father.

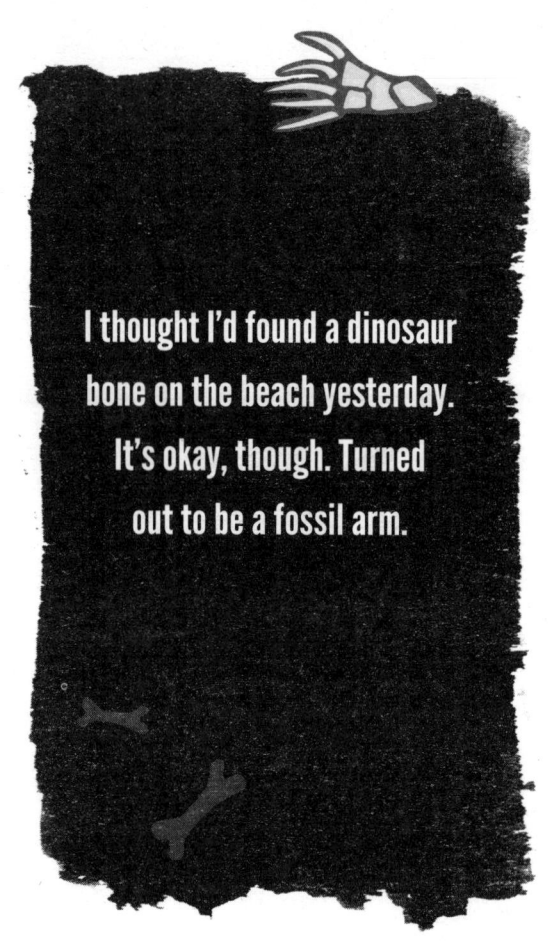

I thought I'd found a dinosaur bone on the beach yesterday. It's okay, though. Turned out to be a fossil arm.

I've always wanted to try crowd-surfing, but I'm worried I might get carried away.

Fun fact!

Jungle music was actually discovered in the jungle in 1843 by explorer Sir Phillip Drummond-Bass.

— ... —

Someone asked me to name two structures that hold water. I was like, 'Well, damn!'

— ... —

Which dogs love science the best?

Labs!

I found a four-leaf clover!
It's a bit creased. I was going to iron it,
but I don't want to press my luck.

I've just signed up to be part of a sleep-study trial, otherwise known as a naptitude test.

I was so close to winning the World's Most Congested Nose title on Saturday, but I blew it.

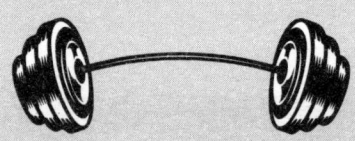

I've decided to quit my job as a personal trainer because the weights are too heavy. I just handed in my too-weak notice.

I've found the cure for my insomnia.
I've made a bed out of rice. I fall asleep
as soon as my head hits the pilau.

I've landed a job at Butterfly World
calculating exactly how many
insects there are.
I'm a mothmatician.

What bird is always out of breath?

A puffin!

My local bakery has started doing deliveries using drones. It all sounds a bit 'pie in the sky' to me.

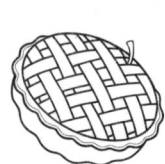

**What's the highest rank in the popcorn army?
Kernel.**

I quit my job as a postman as soon as they handed me my first letter. I looked at it and thought, 'This isn't for me.'

When I have any problems in life,
the first person I go to is my friend
Tommy. Hilfiger something out.

I know a girl who fixes fences.
Her name is Barb Dwyer.

The hospital called and said that my uncle was pronounced dead. I can't believe it. I've been calling him Eddie all these years.

What's the opposite of lady fingers?

Mentos!

A dung beetle walks into a bar and asks the barman, 'Excuse me, is this stool taken?'

I once asked a hotel receptionist for an early morning wake-up call.
She rang me and said, 'It's 6 a.m.! What are you doing with your life?'